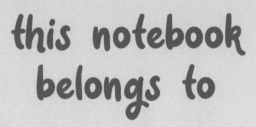

this notebook belongs to

_____

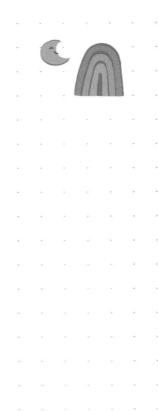

First Rockridge Press trade paperback edition 2022

Rockridge Press and the Rockridge Press logo are trademarks or registered trademarks of Callisto Media Inc. and/or its affiliates in the United States and other countries and may not be used without written permission.

For general information on our other products and services, please contact our Customer Care Department within the United States at (866) 744-2665, or outside the United States at (510) 253-0500.

Paperback ISBN: 978-1-68539-556-8

Manufactured in the United States of America

Interior and Cover Designer: Lisa Realmuto
Art Producer: Maya Melenchuk
Editor: Barbara J. Isenberg
Production Editor: Cassie Gitkin
Production Manager: Riley Hoffman

Illustration © 2022 Ana Sanfelippo

10 9 8 7 6 5 4 3 2 1 0